Between God and Man

By Bob Mumford

LIFECHANGERS®

P.O. Box 3709 ❖ Cookeville, TN 38502
931.520.3730 ❖ lc@lifechangers.org

PLUMBLINE

Published by:

LIFECHANGERS ®
L I B R A R Y   S E R I E S

P.O. Box 3709 | Cookeville, TN 38502
(800) 521-5676 | www.lifechangers.org

All Rights Reserved
ISBN 978-1-940054-16-2

© 2017 Lifechangers
All Rights Reserved
Printed in the United States of America

Between God and Man

By Bob Mumford

"There is no <u>umpire</u> between us, Who may lay his hands upon us both" (Job 9:33).

This Plumbline seeks to serve as a kind of personal gift. It is written in a relational manner that may not be fully understood or embraced if approaching God, Christianity, or Scripture in a soley academic or more cerebral manner. Reception of Christ, in the final analysis, is a subjective and emotional decision. We receive Christ out of personal need, inner hunger not fully identified, and ultimately, with the awareness that things must change in our lives and futures.

The theme itself is so very personal. This concept of conscious Fatherhood has enabled me to abide for more than 60 years. It is foundational, life changing, and will hold you steady in the most complex and difficult of circumstances. Jesus says, "I will never leave you" (Heb. 13:5). He restates that same promise in positive form, "I am with you until the end of the age" (Matt. 28:20).

Christ is the "umpire," called and given the incarnational job description of making God the Father's Love available to this hurting world. Jesus says, "Whoever has seen me has seen the Father" (John 14:9). Thus, Agape is made manifest for the purpose of unconditionally holding on to you and the Father at the exact same time. He is the Umpire standing between God and Man.

Paul states it like this:

What then shall we say to these things? If God is for us, who is against us? He who did not spare His own Son, but delivered Him over for us all, how will He not also with Him freely give us all things? Who will bring a charge against God's elect? God is the one who justifies; who is the one who condemns? Christ Jesus is He who died, yes, rather who was raised, who is at the right hand of God, who also intercedes for us. Who will separate us from the love of Christ? Will tribulation, or distress, or persecution, or famine, or nakedness, or peril, or sword? Just as it is written, "For your sake we are being put to death all day long; We were considered as sheep to be slaughtered." But in all these things we overwhelmingly conquer through Him who loved us. For I am convinced that neither death, nor life, nor angels, nor principalities, nor things present, nor things to come, nor powers, nor height, nor depth, nor any other created thing, will be able to separate us <u>from the love of God, which is in Christ Jesus our Lord</u> (Romans 8:31-39).

There are a multiplicity of things in that passage we should like to engage, the one emphasis we must not miss is that which I have underlined. Christ is God's Love, made incarnate, for the purpose of His being our "umpire," the absolutely urgent person who can keep Father and us relationally together! Simply stated, He will never let you go. The simple issue: Christ is the expression of God's own love to you and me. He cannot, He will not allow His grip on the Father nor the one He has on us to be released. Allow me to say it again: It is God's Love; the Father loves us. Father's love is expressed in the Person of Christ. (2 Cor. 5:19)

The entire Scriptural account, both Old Testament and New Testament, is one of a torrid, complex, and complicated love affair. The first is God's affection and struggle with Israel as a nation. The second reveals the overt failures of the Church, one defection after another. Our theme will seek to put these two issues into proper perspective and provide insight that will serve us in the presence of unpredictable changes that lay ahead. My stated purpose in this Plumbline is to reinforce the necessity of having a working relationship with God as our Father. He is the only one who knows the issues that will face us, and He knows the end from the beginning. Both of these matters will prove to be nothing less than life or death.

My age accompanied by the costly lessons learned as a result of our unusual, rather demanding journey gave birth to this theme. The demands of life have left me with a rather desperate attempt to to write the vision and make it plain. In order to do that, we must begin with an introduction into three kinds of speech, all of which are discovered in the Scripture.

These three languages are:

1. **Mystery**: The effective word here is ineffable. A favorite word of mine that signifies more than rational, meta-physical, beyond our normal ability to comprehend. This implies that at every point we are dependent upon revealed Truth, God revealing Himself and a willingness for us to know Him and His Person.

2. **Metaphor:** This word begins with "meta" signifying a type or manner of speech that is fluid, open, and relational. It is given in parable, analogy, and with human illustration that allows us to see the deeper and more significant meaning. Illustration: "Enoch walked with God" (Genesis 5:24). Such a metaphor has rich, expansive ideas that allow us to enter into the narrative. While the metaphor is true, it refuses to be understood literally, i.e., God and Enoch, holding hands and walking down a dusty road. What we are reaching for in metaphor is relational. Metaphor seeks to draw us into the picture in a participatory manner.

3. **Methodical:** Metaphor is open, relational, and designed to draw us into the happening. Methodical is factual; statements designed to state clear facts and prevent confusion or elusiveness. Facts, which ostensibly, can be understood in alternate ways. The methodical usually ends up as

doctrine or some form of unwritten assumption, usually stiff, declarative and unyielding.

One young person said to me: I do not want a Heavenly Father whose first name begins with "Omni." This may help us illustrate what this burden looks like. Omnipotence or Omniscience, though important, does not encourage or facilitate me to know God as a Father or allow Him to enter my world in a providential manner. Doctrine, however significant, is incapable of moving us into Father's space in a relational manner. This seems to be the central theme of what weighs so heavily upon me. The methodical tends toward inadequacy when seeking to communicate the love affair. As the result of too much methodical, we are "puffed up" as compared to "built up".

The Kingdom offer, when seen in mystery and metaphor is relational and inclusive. It seems to work something like this: We invite Christ into our personal space; He enters in an incarnational manner affirming our forgiveness and acceptance by God the Father. Christ confirms the authenticity of our invitation to be and become an included member of His spiritual family. He implements an efficient mentoring process that establishes in us the joy and skill of learning how to respond to Father's Kingdom offer, more clearly understood as our invitation into His space. This Kingdom offer is clearly presented in 2 Peter 1:11 with the entire chapter as the progressive context. "For in this way the entrance into the eternal kingdom of our Lord and Savior Jesus Christ will be abundantly supplied to you."

If I attempt to convey that relational encounter of the Father and His Kingdom to you in a methodical manner, you may see the implications, even embrace the gift of salvation, and yet fail to successfully enter Father's space—getting to know Him and allowing God the Father to become your providential Father. There is no mystery in our having a Father to whom we have not spoken or been relationally close for many years.

Please note the relational emphasis in Ephesians 1:18. We, as New Testament believers, are identified as "being Father's own inheritance." Our Kingdom relational reality is some of the "reward" Father experiences in the relational reality that the Kingdom has been designed to produce. The relational reality of the love affair Paul attempted to communicate has been dampened or perhaps obscured by the attempt to make it all doctrinal and/or methodical.

Allow me to show you as clearly as I am able the burden of the Lord that seems to press upon me increasingly. "All things work together for good for them that love God" (Romans 8:28). To see this issue as doctrinal is to distort the very life and relational purpose out of its context. To Love God is a relational metaphor. It indicates that we have, because of our affection, made Him first and relate to Him as a Father.

Another biblical example in a similar vein allows us courage to move out of the constraint of rigid doctrine and to enter the relational world of safety and freedom:

> Things which eye has not seen and ear has not heard, and which have not entered the heart of man, all that God has prepared for those who love Him (1 Corinthians 2:9).

The metaphor is able to say more than the methodical is able to tell us. Are we able to observe God's abundant love surging and appealing in a fully relational manner? Can we cease being so sin conscious and begin to be Father conscious allowing Him to enter our space as Father? We are losing control and giving Him that for which He is asking!

In Church history the idea of God as Father loses its personal application and seems relegated to the idea of God as cosmological ruler rather than personal, providential Father. He is both, but we are seeking to rediscover the Father. We have been left with the idea of Fatherhood, but the inner spirit so necessary for authentic Fatherhood to function practically has been essentially lost.

We make a serious mistake if we doctrinally construct Christ to serve as some sort of established goal. He refuses to present Himself as the goal; He is the Way! He came to take us to His Father! It is God in Christ that is bringing an incarnational response that allows us to enter Father's Own Presence with comfort and safety. It is most imperative. "Believe in God, believe also in Me" (John 14:1).

HUMAN CONFUSION BECAUSE WE LOST GOD AS FATHER

What was lost in the encounter at the original defiance? What has caused the loss of the conscious presence of God as a Father? Why do we need an umpire at all? When we are fatherless we are capable of any distortion, unimaginable cruelty, and intentional transgression including blasphemy. A world without the governing reality of God who created it leaves us with a picture similar to a school bus careening down the side of the mountain with no one guiding and the absence of the ability to stop. There is a Swedish word faderlose. I understand it to mean one who has lost their father. Orphan would be the English equivalent.

Here is the question: If we could give the whole world one gift, what would that one gift be? My answer is swift, clear, and emphatic. I would give the human race its Father back! Father God is more than a Savior. The Savior becomes a necessity in order for us to be returned to the Father. Because there is a Father, there is also a Savior!

Such is the relational and metaphoric understanding of Christ's redemptive act. He came not to die but to please His Father, which included dying. His death is for one, urgent purpose: Restore to all humanity the Father that it has grievously lost!

The redemptive act of Christ has been designed to serve in this manner. We must re-examine this idea very closely!

A natural application would cause us to see the same urgency is equally applicable in the human family. All manner of pain, confusion, and defeat has been caused by the failure, cruelty, or absence of a functioning father. Ask any counselor and they will tell you immediately the absence of a father, an abusive father, a non-functioning father can be immediately discerned as the central and obvious cause of present injury. If this lack is the cause of pain and confusion, restoration and presence of Fatherhood speak of healing and wholeness!

FIVE REASONS WE NEED MORE THAN A SAVIOR

Very few people have ever been moved in their behavior by a bible verse! Apart from the love relationship discovered in Fatherhood, demonstrated in the Life of Jesus, moral progress and character appear to be essentially impossible. Here are five reasons (with due acknowledgement to T. C. Edwards, The Epistle to the Hebrews):

1. Our incomplete grasp of the Kingdom and Fatherhood allows the idea of personal savior to become almost an unexamined bumper sticker, minimizing the reality and turning us inward. We

are essentially ignorant of Father's eternal plan. We have not been introduced to what it means to be pleasing to God as a Father. The consequence is an effective and practical departure from the idea of becoming a whole, mature person.

2. The Church seems to move toward existence for the believer's sake. Individuality and personal comfort rule. As a consequence, Church fails to be a Kingdom, governmental prep station advancing Kingdom in all spheres of life, art, science, business, culture, medicine, etc.

3. Increased absence or neglect of engaging Father's purpose and what it means for us to be and become "Father's own inheritance" as stated in Ephesians 1:18. We function as takers and not givers toward God as our Father.

4. Christ is effectively and practically reduced to one who paid a debt for me that I could not pay. Careful examination of this idea reveals an unconscious, self-serving agenda. I am not His family, serving Father's purpose. I have gained an advantage, and now I am guaranteed to go to heaven. The result is haves and have nots.

5. Growth in spiritual purpose as discussed and presented in Hebrews requires spiritual maturity, increased intelligence, and development of character as a pre-requisite to godly behavior. All of this requires us to learn how to please God as a Father. Such is the primary lesson learned in the life of Jesus Christ (See Heb. 5:8).

MORE PROFOUND IMPLICATIONS OF *INCARNATION*

We may be able to see God in Creation and rationalize His Being. However, it is only as we re-examine the redemptive act in a more relational manner that we are enabled to comprehend that God, as a Father, came to us in the Person of Jesus Christ. Now, we are speaking that "other language," one of mystery! Listen, as we seek to put it in context: God was in Christ. Why? To reconcile the world to Himself, restoring His Fatherhood.

When Jesus says, "No one comes to the Father, except by Me" (John 14:6) it is not exclusivism of the Christian message. It is a relational reality. We must avoid methodological language. Incarnation is pure mystery. Listen carefully to what Jesus is saying: "All things have been handed over to Me by My Father; and no one knows the Son except the Father; nor does anyone know the Father except the Son, and anyone to whom the Son wills to reveal Him"(Matthew 11:27).

How necessary and compelling is the beauty of pure mystery! He speaks in a clear and relational manner. No one can know this unless He is willing to reveal it to us. It is on this basis that the spiritual giant C.S. Lewis comes to Christ. He sees that no one and no religion can take Him to the Father. Christ alone is the appointed person. Father has chosen to refuse that privilege to all others!

Allow me to speak the mystery in methodical terms: The Way to the Father is relational, accomplished by Christ as the incarnational route alone. In the Incarnation lies the mystery of knowing God as He seeks to be known, exegeted by the life and ministry of His Incarnate Son (See John 1:18).

How do we get there? What are you trying to say? Why this strong emphasis on the incarnation? In a wonderful theological book entitled New Testament Theology, Joachim Jeremias gives heart-warming insight into the idea of what it means to be able to consciously and authentically address Father as Abba. I considered replicating it here. Another concept follows, equally relationally strengthening, that explains the concept of "unless you are converted and become like little children you will not enter the Kingdom of heaven" (Matthew 18:3). Both of these insights restore Father's personal presence within the actual life of the believer in this present age. Not heaven, not millennial, it is in the now, for you and me!

At my age, as the result of a long and complicated journey, I have been deeply moved. The Father came, personally seeking me. He came in the Person of Christ, through the Holy Spirit, impressing upon me an aspect of His Heart and a hunger to know Him as providential Father. He actually desires to be our providential Father. We can establish this concept with strong scriptural authority, but now we seek to speak in metaphor. Our intent is to draw us into the relational reality, allowing us to cease thinking about our personal failure—imprisoned by our inadequacies, troubled by our idiosyncrasies, and anxious that we have failed to do it correctly.

Father has asked very pointedly for our unshared love, the love that belongs to Him alone. He is asking for our affection! Unconditional affection, given with all of our heart, soul, mind and strength. Approach Him like a little child, learning to say Abba. Do not come in religious terms, to cause Him to accept or like us. Come in deep heart response to the magnificent incarnational reality of our new birth and the entrance of Christ's spirit into our spirit, so that we can say Abba with authenticity and relational freedom! Now, we have actually regained the relationship with our Father, the very one that we had lost.

Joachim Jeremias says, "Only in the sphere of the basileia is God the Father" (New Testament Theology 180). The Greek word requires us to understand basileia as the sphere of God's own governmental reality! This concerns the biblical concept of biblical inheritance in authentic relationship.

This theologian suggests that until and unless we become a "*child again*" (Mt. 18:3) we may experience God's resistance. The possibility exists that we may be refused admittance into Father's space of providentially being governed. Re-read, if you will, Peter's understanding of this, due to his own failure and restoration. His summary in 2 Peter 1:1-11, allows us to experience the relational Way into Father's space in contrast to the doctrinal, methodological understanding. Also see Jesus' explanation in Luke 10:21 where He clarifies and applies this mystery.

Inexplicably, our loss of God as Father also negates and causes loss of an effective mother, for both Father and Mother reside within God's Person. To lose one causes the eventual, unavoidable loss of the other. We become, in metaphorical language, an actual orphan, even though we are a believer in the Person of Christ. We are speaking in terms of mystery!

Hopefully, as the result of this different kind of emphasis, we can cease being so sin conscious and move toward Father conscious, learning to please Him.

HOW THESE THREE LANGUAGES FUNCTION

An attempt to make this practical and workable requires some effort. My heart is for these ideas to break in upon you in a revelatory manner: "Yes, that is what my heart has been searching for!"

Progressively, it looks something like this:

a. Methodology introduces me to the need of metaphor.
b. Metaphor introduces me to the need of mystery.
c. Absence of progression to mystery leaves us lifeless.
d. Lifeless believers live in methodology.

e. We are circling the wagons in futility.
f. Response: Ain't nothing wrong, but something's not right!

We must now make an attempt to grasp the hidden meaning of this parabolic insight. My treasured friend is walking in the back yard with his precocious 7-year-old daughter. A huge blackbird lands on the lower limb of a leafless tree. Suddenly, seeing the food desired, the blackbird flies directly down from the limb to the ground. The daughter says to her father, "The birdie fell." He corrects her, "No, the bird did not fall, he flew down to the ground to be able to eat." She has no insight into aero-dynamics, no mental or emotional capacity for him to explain or make it clear. She repeats her doctrine, "No, daddy, the birdie fell." She now becomes the authority. Note her own pre-supposition is the governing force!

If I could tell you how many times I have insisted that the birdie fell, you would be reluctant to read what I am trying to write! If we refuse the capacity to move from method to metaphor, and on to mystery, we tend toward becoming offended, insistent, demanding, unwilling to consider any other explanation.

God, as our Father, attempts to explain it to us. In order for Him to do that, He is required to wait for us to move into a degree of maturity in which we can hear His voice. That maturity is metaphorical, and then He takes us on into mystery. That is where He lives. He is asking us to enter His space, as a result of His entering ours.

A second illustration of this pivotal point seems to be necessary in order for us to respond with clarity and confidence. I was teaching a fairly large group of leaders that were eager bible-believers but holding a biblical pre-supposition of which I was unaware. This pre-supposition is quite common among some denominations, identified as cessationism, signifying that God has ceased to speak because the biblical canon has now been completed. When examined, it sounds something like this: When the Bible is open, the Lord is speaking. When the Bible is closed, God does not speak.

The class was alive and flowing. The Lord was moving with alacrity and joy. I said, "This morning, in preparation for this class, I felt the Lord say: 'Be sure to make clear emphasis on hearing My Voice.'" When I made this statement the entire class dropped out like a lead balloon! My years of experience allowed me to ask, "What did I say that you do not agree with?" Deathly quiet. No one was willing to speak. Finally, the person who invited me said: "We do not believe the Lord speaks apart from or other than the Scriptures themselves." Strangely enough, the Voice of God is used 5 times in the book of Hebrews alone and used 14x in the Book of John. Voice is used 456x in the Old Testament and New Testament. Hearing and knowing His voice is so foundational that I was astounded. What kind of Father is not allowed to speak?

We are looking at a methodical understanding of

God as a Father. This understanding is set forth as a "safety" issue, provided for new believers who have never crossed a street by themselves. Metaphor and mystery are kept from them because they may hurt themselves and hear a voice that is not God, causing embarrassment to our God or to our church.

We all know that hearing His voice is a skill. No skill is possible that does not allow for mistakes, injuries, and falls. A bit of humor says, the one who learns to ski, hears a voice: "You will fall and rise again many times!"

Listen to the Scripture speak, the very scripture in which they believe with all of their being:

See to it that you do not refuse Him who is speaking. For if those did not escape when they refused him who warned them on earth, much less will we escape who turn away from Him who warns from heaven. And His voice shook the earth then, but now He has promised, saying, "Yet once more I will shake not only the earth, but also the heaven." This expression, "Yet once more," denotes the removing of those things which can be shaken, as of created things, so that those things which cannot be shaken may remain. Therefore, since we receive a kingdom which cannot be shaken, let us show gratitude, by which we may offer to God an acceptable service with reverence and awe; for our God is a consuming fire (Hebrews 12:25-29).

We must see that this Kingdom is moving toward a time in history when all that we know and understand will be shaken. All that is religious and earthly will be shaken in a manner that will cause us to choose God's Kingdom. We will be required to know and embrace His Kingdom reality. God, as a Father, is a Consuming Fire. We have identified choosing the Kingdom as learning to make the third choice. Maturity is having learned to hear His voice in contrast to the multiplicity of voices that are insisting on being heard.

Departing from that which is childish and seeking to function in that which is child-like is the skill we pursue. "When I was a child, I spoke as a child. When I became a man, I put away childish things." Childish may not actually be wrong, simply increasingly inadequate. That which we have embraced is not sufficiently mature to meet our present needs. We require a Father to guide, correct, and instruct. For that to be a Kingdom reality, we must be willing to embrace God, as a Father.

FIVE INSIGHTS MOVING US TOWARD BIBLICAL MATURITY

1. William Paul Young, author of this disturbing book entitled *The Shack,* writes to intentionally shake us in a manner we have described. He writes 80%+ in metaphor and mystery. With shock and awe, I read and re-read this unpretentious manuscript. He helped thousands to move out

of the prison of pre-supposition and mundane methodology into metaphor and then plunged his reader into mystery with effectiveness.

He seemed to offend as many as he helped. Disturbing responses filled the air. Internal resistance was discovered within the Body of Christ. Personally, I was positively moved in a way that was difficult to explain. I spoke of this publicly, only to be deluged with Christians that dissented.

This principle seems to be aligned with our theme. He sought to move us out of method, into metaphor and mystery. God is Spirit. Father is not an old man with a white beard, sitting in the heavens. God "hides Himself" (Isa. 45:15). God is mystery.

We are required to return to the daughter in the back yard who thought the birdie fell. We discovered that we do not know aero-dynamics. All we know is: It is not possible for God to be represented like that; God is not like that! Now we are stewing, unable to make sense of all that is coming down.

2. *Our expanding universe*. Isaac Newton lived in the 1700's, some two hundred years after Copernicus and Galileo established the heliocentric solar system, and he was responsible for pioneering many fine points of orbital mechanics. Isaac Newton, with great accuracy, explained the Universe to us. It was very methodical! When

we speed ahead a few hundred years, we discover that Newton's universe is not only expanding, it contains trillions of galaxies of which we knew little or nothing. Suddenly, we are introduced to a new science, insights that seem to function on something close to faith. New science now introduces us to quarks, chaos, fractals, fourteen dimensions, string theory, and other discoveries and possibilities that blow the natural mind. Such is mystery. Such is the necessity of science now speaking in metaphor, almost incapable of communicating that which science now perceives. God's created Kingdom has been understood as far too finite and limited. Father is forcing us out of our comfort level into His space of metaphor and mystery.

3. *God's Own Person.* When we have finished reading and studying all of the doctrine of God, it remains inadequate, less than what has needed to be said. Father is more than, greater than, other than all that has been explained. I have owned hundreds of books that professed to explain the mystery. Once, as a young pastor, I actually said: "This morning, I am going to speak on the Mystery of the Kingdom. When I am finished, it will no longer be mystery for all of you!"

4. *Kingdom mystery* may eventually require us to consider the fact that Christ's baptism was far more complex and earth shattering than any of us could possibly imagine. It may be possible that

His water baptism and His Spirit baptism carried cosmic implications. Cosmic signifies the world system in ordered form. There is a real possibility that Jesus was buried in water for the distinct purpose of His being buried as a Jewish/Hebrew Messiah and resurrected as the cosmic Christ whose job description was the greater fulfillment of Father's Promise to Abraham: In you, Abraham, all of the families of the earth will be blessed (See Genesis 22:18). This transcends my methodical understanding of Jesus the Messiah and nearly causes biblical shock! Once we are willing to consider all it means for Christ to fulfill and implement Father's Promise to Abraham, we may then be open to a cosmic Christ and a global Kingdom agenda.

5. *The Message* as a New Testament translation may help enable us to modify the methodical. As a Greek student, I was offended at the liberty Peterson used in translating the Greek words. I was so trapped in the literal, it made me unable to see and hear anything that was not academic and grammatically accurate. For instance: *"Take my yoke and learn of me"* became "*Learn the unforced rhythms of Grace*" (Matthew 11:29). It took direct effort to grasp the beauty and reasoning. Under duress from what I think was the Lord, I was listening to *The Message* in audio form. It was speaking to me in a manner that made me cringe. I was hearing things that were metaphorical

and mystery for the very first time. Another example: *"'I say to you', says Jesus, 'that the whores and the robbers will enter the Kingdom before you'"* (Matthew 21:31). I was so shocked that I sat up in the chair and took off the headphones to grab the text. I have always encouraged others to read several translations for the ability to see into the text more deeply. *The Message* may begin to serve us in this manner.

THE FATHER HIMSELF: INSIGHT INTO OUR BIBLICAL EMPHASIS

What I seek to accomplish in this section is focused on the necessity of intentionally finding God as our own Father. I do not mean in a redemptive sense. I am speaking of a conscious effort to embrace God as providential Father. We are required to invite Him into our own personal space!

The question that God, as Father, may not have asked you yet goes something like this: Do you want Me to govern you as a sovereign King or a providential Father? The ramifications are world-shaking. Either way, we are going to be governed. It is choosing the manner in which His government is being exercised. If we choose God as providential Father and refuse to listen, respond, and function as His child, the governing factor reverts back to the sovereign manner. Refusing His Fatherhood comes at a cost!

Intentionally and consciously inviting God to be

in your space as a Father, has multiple implications. He actually is, amazingly enough, willing to do that! However, it is compulsory for us to make the needed adjustments as to how this actually works.

Note the following scriptures in this light. Please take the time needed to absorb the intended purpose. Note the repeated statement: "the Father Himself."

For I did not speak on My own initiative, but the Father Himself who sent Me has given Me a commandment as to what to say and what to speak. I know that His commandment is eternal life; therefore the things I speak, I speak just as the Father has told Me (John 12:49–50).

For the Father Himself loves you, because you have loved Me and have believed that I came forth from the Father (John 16:27).

Now may our God and Father Himself and Jesus our Lord direct our way to you; and may the Lord cause you to increase and abound in love (Agape) for one another, and for all people, just as we also do for you; so that He may establish your hearts without blame in holiness before our God and Father at the coming of our Lord Jesus with all His saints (1 Thessalonians 3:11–13).

For this reason therefore the Jews were seeking all the more to kill Him, because He not only was breaking the Sabbath, but also was calling God His own Father, making Himself equal with God. Therefore Jesus answered and was saying to them, "Truly, truly, I say to you, the Son can do nothing of Himself, unless it is something He sees the Father doing; for whatever the Father does, these things the Son also does in like manner (John 5:18–19).

When scripture is read from a spiritual perspective in contrast to a redemption centered on heaven, we discover that it is His own desire to be our personal Father in this present life. "*Our Father…*" (Matthew 6:9) expresses desire for a covenantal relationship, one of love and care, established by God. Thus, "*Our Father…*" is a fulfillment of the Old Testament expectations.

This spiritual reality seems to depend upon our recognition and consequent cultivation of such a relational up-grade. Note how this is presented: "'And I will be a Father to you, and you shall be sons and daughters to Me,' Says the Lord Almighty" (2 Corinthians 6:18). How could He declare Himself any more directly?

What then does it mean for the entire human family to lose their father? How does Father's repeated request for us to love Him with all of our heart, soul, mind, and strength speak to us? All of the Old Testament promises of Fatherhood are now being fulfilled in the Person of Jesus Christ. Compare: Luke 12:32: "Do not be afraid, little flock, for your Father has chosen gladly to give you the kingdom." And Mt. 6:10: "For it is not you who speak, but it is the Spirit of your Father who speaks in you."

We are able to confirm and present this theme with strength and confidence by reason of Jesus' own statements, "Stop clinging to Me, for I have not yet ascended to the Father; but go to My brethren and say to them, 'I ascend to My Father and your Father, and My God and your God'" (John 20:17). "Then the righteous will shine forth as the sun in the kingdom of their Father" (Matthew 13:43).

HEARING HIS VOICE MAY DETERMINE LIFE OR DEATH

"You shall not have any other gods before Me" (Exodus 20:3). When we engage the loss of Father concept correctly, we discover something that is frightening and inexorable: I am the little god! What is involved is that I love myself more than I love God, more than I love others, or in the realm of suicide loving myself more than life itself! Quietly hidden in our internal resistance lay a secret fortress that we have carefully constructed since childhood. No one knows its potency but you and God. When we discover ourselves in unresolved conflict, we escape into this secret, internal refuge for protection. It is poorly constructed and inadequate. We seem to have the confidence that it will serve our escape needs, but this internal refuge will be shaken.

Our loving Father knows about our secret hide-out, and He efficiently moves us toward dismantling this secret refuge. With wisdom and care, He seeks to persuade us to make Him to be our hiding place. The Father was the refuge to which Christ retreated. It is that same Father that Christ seeks to reveal. He desires to encourage us to choose Him, in exchange for the refuge we have constructed. He will forgive as many times as is necessary. However, He will never cease to move us toward our own personal freedom.

No other gods before Him? He does not and will not force, pressure, or demand. He does know how to present life in the category of "all things," allowing us to see Him and His provision. The voice of the accuser suggests, "If you yield your secret place, God may ask for something you are unprepared to give."

I am experiencing some degree of reluctance just identifying this biblical reality. I am the problem, yet He loves me without reserve. Nothing can separate me from God's Own care. Christ won for us the freedom, which gives the confidence to dismantle this very common but super-secret hiding place. Returning to the Father, without reservation or fear constitutes a serious challenge. One that will require implementation of all that we have presented. We really do need a Father who knows and cares!

I am not asking for you to trust religion or people. I am asking you to get serious about the secret hide out. He has been unfairly represented, attacked, and falsely accused. When Jesus asks the twelve "Have you lacked anything?" (Luke 22:35), His intent is to cultivate the trust and openness with God as a Father upon which He has built His life and ministry.

We may, at this juncture, need to learn a new word: acquiesce. It means to give in with reluctance. God as a Father lives like that. He acquiesces in our relationships. Wanting us to be open and full of trust He yields, accepts, and works around our ever-present fears, idiosyncrasies, and phobias that keep us in bondage. He seeks to set us free! All of this depends upon our choice, gaining that freedom that belongs to us as His very own relational family.

Father Himself, walked out into His own perfect freedom in the Person of His Son. He is free to love us and do so in mystery. He provided everything necessary for us to walk into greater freedom when He inseminated us with His own DNA in the new birth. His purpose has been our freedom from our greatest idol, love for self. This causes us to carefully guard our secret refuge.

His freedom penetrates everything. We cannot know Life as He intended when we are occupied with obsessive, controlling fears and demands that produce spiritual death. Repeated forgiveness does not produce the freedom that yields life.

God is Light. God is Agape. He is above all, a

Father. Christ, above all, is our Shepherd bringing us to His Father. The baptism in the Holy Spirit has been identified as "the Promise of the Father." He has repeated the promises, emphasized the security, and re-affirmed His appeal with various guarantees of His faithfulness; He demonstrated it in the Life and ministry of Jesus Christ. Now, Christ asks us to follow Him as He takes us to His Father on this exciting, demanding, and deeply rewarding journey.

Benediction

> *Now the God of peace, who brought up from the dead the great Shepherd of the sheep through the blood of the eternal covenant, even Jesus our Lord, equip you in every good thing to do His will, working in us that which is pleasing in His sight, through Jesus Christ, to whom be the glory forever and ever. Amen (Hebrews 3:20).*

LIFECHANGERS ®

P.O. Box 3709 ❖ Cookeville, TN 38502
931.520.3730 ❖ lc@lifechangers.org

www.ingramcontent.com/pod-product-compliance
Lightning Source LLC
Chambersburg PA
CBHW060044040426
42331CB00032B/2387